Pastoring

Past(
on Empty

DR. THOMAS A. WEBB
FOREWORD BY DR. FREDRICC GERARD BROCK
Former NFL Linebacker for the Houston Texans
Lead Pastor of The Message Church San Antonio, Texas

Pastoring on Empty

Published by Lee's Press and Publishing Company
www.LeesPress.net

A Premiere Self-Publishing
Services Company

ISBN-13: 979-8-9896434-7-9

PAPERBACK

Table of Contents

Acknowledgments

There is a host of leaders within the Body of Christ who have tremendously impacted my life and Christian ministry as a leader and later as a pastor over the past thirty years. These individuals serving in Christian ministry have helped shape who I am as a person and as a man of God.

To my Father, Rev. Alfred Webb, thank you, sir, for encouraging me since I was nineteen years old when I shared with you, mom, and the pastor of our church that God called me to preach his Word. During my period of struggle in my early years to prepare myself for the call, both your and mom's prayers sustained me. Thank you for the many lessons you taught me about intestinal fortitude and never giving up.

In remembrance of Apostle Ancil Carruthers, former Founder and Pastor of Holy Revival Center of Altus, Oklahoma, who, as an older pastor, saw something in me I did not see in myself in my early twenties. He pastored and trained me in an old country church in rural Altus, Oklahoma. He infused in me the importance of prayer, continuous study of the Word, and proper interpretation of the biblical text, with a strong emphasis on Holiness. I have never forgotten the many lessons he taught me personally and across the pulpit.

To Bishop James Black, Founder and Senior Pastor of Faith Tabernacle of Praise of Biloxi, Mississippi, who afforded me the opportunity to serve under his great leadership. His continuous encouragement and instruction concerning exercising our faith in God has yielded great dividends in ministry and throughout my life. As a senior leader in the Body of Christ who has prospered in church leadership and business enterprising, helped me to recognize the early signs of ministry burnout. Bishop Black taught me to consistently ask for God's wisdom and direction to further alleviate burnout in ministry.

To Dr. Janice Martin, Founder and Senior Pastor of The Book

1

of Acts Tabernacle of Praise of Wichita, Kansas, and a strong prophetic voice within the Body of Christ who has made an indelible impact on my life and ministry when I was at a point of burnout on a few occasions much earlier during my earlier years of serving in the pastorate. Through her strong prophetic ministry and love for pastors who are hurting and have left the ministry, she possesses the anointing to speak life to dying visions within pastors. Her ability to educate and equip church leaders for end-time ministry throughout the body of Christ is paramount for clarity of God's purpose and will for mankind throughout the earth. The anointing she possesses to speak God's word of healing to pastors and clergy has provided hope for them cross-denominationally and globally.

To Bishop B. Courtney McBath, Founder and Senior Pastor of Calvary Revival Church and leader of the Calvary Leaders Network of Norfolk, Virginia, who in my earlier years of pastoring taught me the need to add value to the call of God in my life in seeking and obtaining higher academic education throughout my pastorate. Doing this would further equip me to preach and teach in a scholarly way to God's people. God would illuminate understanding in the minds, hearts, and lives of God's people and usher sinners to our Lord. Bishop McBath instilled in me that "Leaders who serve are leaders who lead."

To Dr. D. Myles Golphin, Visionary of the Living in Favor Global Network of Raleigh, North Carolina, who graciously availed himself and his ministry to me throughout the last two decades. He has been a prominent leader and theologian in my life since my first pastorate in Rocky Mount, North Carolina in the late 1990s. I was honored to have sat in numerous classes he taught in the areas of the episcopacy, graduate-level academics, and hermeneutics of God's Word. He instilled in me the continuous need during the propagation of God's Word to immerse oneself in the biblical text like a time machine and encourage God's people through multisensory teaching and preaching.

2

To Bishop Lyle and Pastor Deborah Dukes of Harvest Life Church of Woodbridge, Virginia, who infused in me to lead and exhibit a Spirit of Excellence in ministry, to operate with a strong administrative acumen in the local church, and "to be willing to evangelize and win souls to the Kingdom of God wisely." They both, as world-class leaders within the Body of Christ, instilled in me the importance of the willingness to take the next step, regardless of what it looks like, through faith and trust in God to lead by the Holy Spirit. The immediate military connection I experienced with the Dukes was comforting and understanding as it pertains to the will of God and transitions. The anointing and spiritual gift of faith they both operate in has spilled over into the lives of countless pastors and church leaders globally.

To Dr. Lorenzo Peterson Senior Bishop of the International Alliance Communion of McDonough, Georgia, who has afforded me the opportunity to teach leaders within his organization in the areas of bereavement ministry and pastoral burnout. His organization of pastors and church leaders to lead cutting-edge churches and ministries through the anointing he possesses in ecclesial leadership has catapulted many pastors to new areas of hope and encouragement to lead their local churches and ministries. The anointing and spiritual gift he possesses of emphasizing the need for spiritual governments mentioned in 1 Corinthians 12:28 has brought an uplifting and encouraging spirit to countless pastors and ministers globally who serve under his leadership. The perceptive ability God gifted him to see in leaders what they cannot see in themselves through his evangelistic and motivational preaching has ushered healing and understanding in the lives of pastors and church leaders globally.

To Apostle Walter Barbour, Founder and Senior Pastor of Victory Faith Center of Goldsboro, North Carolina, who has served as a spiritual father to me in the areas of the need to walk in the Spirit of Wisdom and sound counsel for those who are hurting. The teaching anointing he possesses has helped launch me forward into areas of academic research and the study of pastoral burnout and how it affects marital relationships. It has been an honor to have received God-ordained opportunities to be mentored and spiritually sharpening from this Man of God. The impact he has made on me is continuing to aid me in better serving and leading as a pastor. Encouragement regarding the ascension gifts of Ephesians 4:11-13, our purpose, and why we add value to the Body of Christ has helped clarify my role and stance spiritually in the church and outside of military ministry.

To Superintendent Pastor James and Evangelist Dawn Tharrington of Evangel Church of God in Christ of Reidsville, North Carolina, who have served as a spiritual big brother and big sister to me since my late teens, when I answered the call to Christian Ministry. They have served as role models to me in ministry and have interceded in prayer for me during critical transitions in my life. The Tharringtons' have always shared accurate and timely Words from the Lord with and for me, which have changed my life forever. The mentoring, motivational spirit, and prophetic anointing they both possess for this end-time generation of X and Y youth on fire for Christ is much needed to aid in health and healing for the hurting and misunderstood.

To Pastor Cedric, Prophetess Virginia McCabe, and the House of Prayer Ministries of Fayetteville, North Carolina, who have served as pivotal contributors to my spiritual strength throughout the years. Not only have Pastor Cedric, Prophetess Virginia McCabe, and I served in ministry together, but we are also family. Thank you for being in my corner during some of the most difficult times of my pastoral ministry and personal life. You both have spoken God's prophetic words of strength to congregations I have led both in and out of the military, to my family, and to me on numerous occasions. Thank you for being the vessels God uses to usher an end-time renewal of hope and strength to the Body of Christ.

To Chaplain, Colonel Matthew Franke, my former boss two

different times in two different locations in our world, who has encouraged me to maintain my health and lead teams in the same spirit. The spirit of organization and diligence of leadership impacted my life greatly when I was a young company-grade officer in the Air Force. The many lessons of leadership have aided me during my seasons of leadership over teams both small and large. I will never forget the fireside chats Chaplain Franke and I would have with our teams to take note of times we encountered breaking points that led to burnout. His gift of military writing has aided me and countless members of the military.

To Dr. Clyde Dyson, Chaplain, Lieutenant Colonel (USAF Retired), who has known me for most of my career as an Air Force Chaplain both in the Reserves and active duty. God has certainly used him as his mouthpiece during his years of active-duty and post active-duty service. His consistent encouragement, wisdom, instruction, and prophetic insight have served as resources of inspiration for me. His spiritual gift of discerning spirits has aided me in the areas of prayer and discernment in God's will during my times of burnout and bereavement.

Dedication

This book is dedicated to all pastors and clergy members who are presently experiencing, have experienced, or may potentially experience burnout. God gave me the vision to share with you some real-life information, along with experiences from burnout. I will also share my academic research with practical examples of those who have served in a ministerial capacity, to reveal the commonality of burnout experienced by professionals in all facets of ministry. If you are presently experiencing symptoms of burnout, allow me to talk you through your experience. I want to support you through this book during your late nights when you are not able to sleep, or during the day when you are at a standstill mentally and feel like giving up. To those who feel like they just can't do it anymore, my prayer for you is that this book serves as an inspirational resource with answers for why you should not give up.

Foreword

In the complex tapestry of our society, clergy members stand as pillars, offering guidance, solace, and spiritual nourishment to those in need. Dr. Thomas Webb's insightful exploration of the challenges faced by pastors in his book on clergy burnout is a timely and crucial contribution to our understanding of the immense responsibilities that these civic advisors carry. In my twenty-five years of ministry, I have found that pastoral burnout is not just exhaustion of the body and mind; it's weariness of the soul, a silent cry for rest amid relentless service.

By the nature of their calling, clergy members engage daily with diverse individuals, addressing a spectrum of concerns ranging from counseling and spiritual observances to leading worship services and advocating for social justice. The vitality they bring to their roles profoundly impacts not only the individuals they serve but also the communities and society at large.

Dr. Webb begins by unraveling the concept of burnout, delving into its nuanced dimensions, and illustrating how it manifests in the lives of pastors. Burnout, as a persistent and harmful mindset associated with one's work, is explored through the lens of tiredness, stress, diminished impetus, and the development of malfunctioning behaviors and actions. The author skillfully connects these theoretical underpinnings to the unique challenges clergy members face: diminished energy, reduced personality, perception of dependence and hopelessness, and the emergence of undesirable and sarcastic mindsets.

The multifaceted responsibilities inherent in the role of a pastor make pastors particularly susceptible to burnout, a reality underscored by research in the field. Dr. Webb sheds light on the vulnerability's pastors face, emphasizing the profound impact clergy burnout can have on the individuals themselves, the churches they lead and pastor, and, by extension, the broader populations they serve.

What distinguishes this book is Dr. Webb's commitment to grounding the discussion in real-life examples drawn from his academic research. The narratives shared within these pages offer a poignant and authentic portrayal of clergy members' challenges, allowing readers to connect with the human experience behind the theories.

As readers embark on this journey through the pages of Dr. Webb's work, they are invited to reflect on the profound message encapsulated in Matthew 11:28—an invitation to find rest for the weary. This book is not just an academic exploration of burnout; it is a compassionate guide, a source of insight, and a beacon of hope. Dr. Webb extends a prayer to all readers that, through the Holy Spirit's illumination, their understanding will be deepened, their minds opened to the causes of burnout, and their hearts moved toward prevention and recovery.

May this book serve as a valuable resource for clergy members, congregations, and all those who seek to support and understand the challenges faced by those called to serve. In the pursuit of preventing and healing from burnout, may the wisdom shared within these pages foster resilience, renewal, and a deeper appreciation for the dedicated individuals who bear the weight of spiritual leadership.

Dr. Fredricc Gerard Brock
Former NFL Linebacker for the Houston Texans
Lead Pastor of The Message Church in San Antonio, Texas.

Introduction

Clergy members are crucial civic advisors who work together with many people daily and, in some cases, on a routine basis. The vitality that they carry to their job can impact other individuals through various approaches, including counseling, spiritual observances, regular weekly worship services, and social justice issues. This chapter presents a brief overview of pastors who may suffer burnout. Burnout is a stress-related theory that is classified as a persistent, harmful mindset associated with one's work that is primarily characterized by tiredness, but also includes stress, lessened impetus, and the advancement of malfunctioning behaviors and actions (Els et al., 2015).

For pastors, this is described as resulting in diminished energy, reduced personality, perception of dependence and despondency, as well as the expansion of undesirable and sarcastic mindsets (Brewer, 2016). Burnout may happen because the clergy member is viewed as an influential person with many responsibilities. Clergy deficiency, reduced efficacy, and stress have numerous adverse influences on clergy representatives, the churches they lead and pastor, and larger populations. Pastors are more vulnerable to experience burnout than individuals from other occupations because of their various responsibilities in leading, preaching, teaching, counseling in the religious setting and in society (Baruth et al., 2014).

Without realizing it, we can succumb to burnout. The goal in this book is to share some real-life examples from my academic research on what clergy members and pastors face when it comes to burnout. As you take the time to read this book, my prayer for you is that you allow the Holy Spirit to illuminate your understanding and open your mind to the causes of burnout, how to prevent it, and how to recover from it. Matthew 11:28: "Come to Me, all you who labor and are heavy laden, and I will give you rest."

CHAPTER ONE

Clergy Burnout and How it Affects the Pastor

"I'm Overwhelmed!"

Clergy Burnout and the Job Description

Burnout is recognized as a widespread problem among pastors, across denominational lines and in multiple church sizes (White, 2020). Burnout is described as energy reduction without proportionate repair, and it results from the endless complications, requirements, and expectations frequently undergone by clergy members and pastors (Chandler, 2009). When burnout began to be researched and examined in the 1970s, studies were principally for those working in human health care services, social workers, and emergency responders (Schaufeli, et al., 2009). As a comparison for the sapping of an individual's energy, burnout implies the suffocating of a blaze of fire with a form of extinguisher (Marcena, 2018).

It means that once a fire is active, it cannot stay lit unless there is sufficient fuel to keep it ablaze. Over a period of time, clergy members who experience burnout lose the vivacity to continue making an effective impact on a congregation. Unfortunately, the clergy member will not accomplish much to their satisfaction in ministry, their church, and their community. In other words, the clergy member's capability to serve is tested and proven to the point that the clergy member experiences fatigue that impacts their work in the church (Marcena, 2018).

Clergy burnout causes the pastor or minister to question their calling —in both ministry outside of a church setting, and ministry to those in the church setting. If they do not channel their quest for knowledge and seek help when in the stage of pastoral burnout, it can cause them to leave the ministry (Muse et al., 2016). It is possible that a clergy member could be matched with the wrong church in terms of doctrinal viewpoints, which can lead to conflict with church staff and parishioners (Bassford, 2008). Pastors encounter countless situations that can lead to pastoral burnout in the roles they serve (Clay, 2019).

The job description of a clergy member incorporates many

distinct roles which they may serve simultaneously within a day, thereby creating an excessive workload. Clergy preside over funerals and memorial services, provide counseling, and assist with marriages in decline, all of which can be overwhelming (Adams et al., 2016). In some cases, clergy are viewed as an extension of the professional mental health community. Clergy members attempt to generate a collective vision for the church and preside over the church staff and members at large, most of whom serve as volunteers, to bring the vision into focus. Clergy also have been regarded as the best resource for lower socioeconomic echelons of the population who cannot afford professional counseling (Lebo, 2020).

A reason clergy deal with burnout is the vagueness of the role they serve, which is due to unclear objectives and expectations (Fee, 2018). Many pastors do not believe seminary education and training primed them to take the lead and collaborate with interagency partners in their towns and cities. Not every pastor has clear job expectations or a clear job description, so as a result, many of them operate the way they feel is best for them. The clergy are expected to serve in various roles such as pastor, teacher, counselor, sermon preparer, educator at their church, and servant in the community (Gill et al., 2018). Given the individuality of clergy familiarity, it is significant to hypothesize burnout as a condition that permits for knowledge of a person's emotions, whether positive or negative (Lebo, 2020).

The Role of Senior Pastor

Senior pastors have one of the highest-caring professions that experience burnout. Senior pastors are often in high demand. These individuals are expected to communicate effectively through teaching and preaching, to understand all the theological implications of the Bible in the world, to be a loving and caring counselor, to excel as a business manager and administrator, to be the public relations expert for the community, to provide mentoring and supervision to other staff, and to lead effectively. Juggling these many responsibilities can be a burden, and burnout is a state of mind of those who serve in professions in which they provide care (Burnette, 2016).

Burnout may be especially prevalent within passionate, caring occupations, and pastoring a church is one of those occupations (Burnette, 2016). As a result, burnout affects individuals in many different professions that are focused on helping others, but the role of senior pastor lends itself to burnout. It is difficult for a pastor to gauge the challenging work they have put into leading a church congregation. For their legacy to be legitimate to them, they must quantify the church's spiritual growth while the church is concurrently growing numerically, which is a difficult task (Ream, 2016).

The pastor's job is one in which there is constant repetition that can result in fatigue, and this in turn can lead to exhaustion and dullness. A pastor interacts with people who expect a great deal of them and their time. Impractical, vague, and unspecified anticipations can lead to unmet hopes, struggle, consternation, culpability, and foiling resulting in fatigue (Ream, 2016). Burnout and fatigue amongst clergy can be a risk to the local church's well-being and vivacity (Dowson et al., 2010).

Pastors serve the same congregation of people yearly by choice, which includes those who are difficult to lead and pastor. They spend a lot of time with those who are impoverished economically or in spirit. Those people that the pastor spends time investing in, who choose not to change, can create moments that are discouraging and disheartening. The pastor leads those who come to church to have their spiritual needs met. The parishioners need to feel important, and they need to address how they feel in addition to their many responsibilities. When these parishioners do not receive the responsiveness, they believe is due to them, they can become indignant and spiteful. The pastor then must resist the temptation to operate in their guise (Ream, 2016).

The Effects of Burnout

The three effects of burnout are emotional exhaustion, outward depersonalization, and most of all the lack of personal accomplishment one feels internally (Angus, 2016). Jethro, Moses's father-in-law, gave Moses great advisement and counsel in Exodus 18:13–27. This is often referred to by ministry professionals as "The Jethro Principle." Moses provided advisement to him as the people waited for his counsel from morning to evening. Jethro, Moses's father-in-law noticed that if Moses continued to do this, he would burn out. He gave Moses' advisement in the delegation of judges who could handle the load of counseling. Moses did as Jethro advised, and it lightened his load. It is crucial to comprehend exactly how burnout affects clergy members (Adams, 2017). Individuals suffering from burnout report lesser concentrations of job contentment and have greater stress levels than persons who are not suffering burnout (Pickett et al., 2017). Clergy members who have suffered burnout often reveal to their cohorts and those they serve that they are burned out. They may show it through their character with impropriety and indecisiveness, which further implicates burnout levels in parishioners and church staff members.

Burnout is an occupation-associated condition evident in its symptoms of poignant fatigue, lack of achievement, and feelings of detachment from working to support those who suffer from working to support others suffering from it. It generally arises from persistent relational effort with others in a caregiving role, particularly with those who have difficulties or are distressed. Social ministry workers may be at certain risk for experiencing fatigue due to exhausting most of their time tending to or being present for other people (Pickett et al., 2017). The term "burnout" was first used to refer to electrical fires (Sanford, 1982) and was not related to any human emotion or situation (Angus, 2016). Maslach and Jackson (1981) defined burnout as a state of physical, emotional, and mental fatigue that leads to the misery that affects personal relationships. Other peripheral

15

effects of burnout, along with fatigue, are lack of motivation and unexplained bodily issues such as headaches, digestive issues, and periods of unexpected outbursts from the person experiencing burnout.

The need to study pastoral burnout is vital, as pastors and clergy in various leadership positions suffer in silence. Still, the silence is frequently a result of the burnout that is causing them to feel frustration, inadequacy, and a lack of motivation to fully serve as they could. In some instances, burnout can refer to lessened motivational vigor to complete tasks. Despite increased pastoral duty, staff decreases seem inevitable to a generation of American churches that have lived through downscaling and efficacy-related measures. Today's pastor, recognized as a willing servant, oftentimes has added obligations such as overseeing church property, instructing programs, running volunteer staff functions while also supervising them, and accomplishing copious organizational responsibilities (Hessell, 2015). Burnout is a disease no one talks about until it is too late.

Burnout is a state a person is put in due to their emotional, spiritual, social, physical, and emotional exhaustion. This is caused by prolonged and extreme quantities of strain, which cause a person's body to create adrenaline. It precludes them from seeing their capabilities and the importance of their vocation (Strong, 2017). Pastors and clergy members should seek resources when they are mentally and physically depleted so they may recover from emotional exhaustion. As they are constantly caring for others, burnout is a possible consequence if they do not receive adequate support and replenishment for their own well-being (Muse et al., 2016). Those pastors who struggle under pressure in life may have to cope with tragic situations, lack of hierarchical church support, and low or no recognition for achievements, which can all affect a clergy member to the extent that they succumb to burnout (Williams, 2019).

Burnout denotes a deterioration in vigor, enthusiasm, and obligation. It happens when significant accomplishments do not come to completion, particularly in work settings of poor pay and deprived acknowledgment of labors (Barnard & Curry, 2012). Burnout also occurs when a person cares very much for people and their care is not reciprocated to contribute to the replenishment of the caregiver's physical, mental, and spiritual faculties (Muse et al., 2016). Pastors and clergy members can take on too many roles in the community, leading to burnout when they do not consider their responsibilities to the churches and ministry positions, they provide ministry in.

Burnout often challenges pastors and clergy, which also puts them in a state of frustration, especially when they feel that the work, they are doing is not getting the results they intended. Pastors and clergy are likely more susceptible to burnout than persons from other professions because of the numerous and diverse roles they serve in the church and community (Baruth et al., 2014). Research has examined why they experience burnout and has shown that pastors suffer from it as a result of emotional exhaustion, job dissatisfaction, self-blame, incapacity to meet budgetary and payroll requirements, criticism, ministry embarrassment, and culpability (Crosskey et al., 2015). We all deal with and experience burnout at various levels. It does not matter if you are a pastor or a clergy member of some sort.

Pastors may be predisposed to fatigue if they do not create time to reestablish their concentration and energy (Hebden, 2020). The pastor can endure burnout from a lot of emotional exhaustion, depersonalization, compassion fatigue, loneliness, lack of personal accomplishment, and the 24/7 mentality. I sought to ascertain the ministry experiences of pastors who served churches while they were in the burnout stage. As pastors ministered to their churches, they were prone to burnout, but how they dealt with it and moved forward was paramount for this study. Also, the opportunity to learn of the actual lived experiences of clergy and pastoral members was essential to gain insight into the journey of the burnout stage.

Emotional Exhaustion

The first gauge of burnout is emotional exhaustion (Frederick et al., 2018). It is the fundamental stress element of burnout, and it reduces a person's emotional and physical means (Hough et al., 2019). Emotional exhaustion entails feelings of being emotionally overstretched and drained (Dunbar et al., 2018). A person who experiences emotional exhaustion can sense and operate with a lack of energy which inhibits their ability to relax (Dunbar et al., 2018). Pastors go through periods of emotional exhaustion when they have administrative demands, or are counseling members, and need to respond to the other obligations at the church (Whiting, 2017).

Mental fatigue, for pastors who experience it, can make it difficult to focus on those they lead in the parish. Due to the difficult nature of their occupation, clergy members can be vulnerable to mental fatigue and the exhaustion of their capability to sustain responsiveness (Gill et al., 2018). Thus, clergy who provide counseling services may experience emotional and mental exhaustion. Such duties require concentration and wisdom to serve the congregation and others (Stephens, 2020) adequately and professionally. Moreover, the cleric can become fearful of the number of emails, phone calls, faxes, notes, and letters. These can become a major drain on their energy and spirit (Schaefer & Jacobsen, 2009).

Clergy who consistently provide counseling may experience emotional and mental exhaustion. These responsibilities involve attentiveness and knowledge to serve the church (Stephens, 2020) sufficiently and professionally. Burnout is also considered when a person experiences emotional exhaustion and spiritual and mental fatigue which causes a person's body to overproduce adrenaline. As a result, the person begins to question their ability to succeed in their work (Strong, 2017). When pastors experience emotional exhaustion during burnout, church staff and members should afford the opportunity for pastors to receive benefits in the areas of vacations, sabbaticals, and retreats to assist pastors in taking care of themselves. Vacations have been demonstrated to have restorative benefits. Annual retreats organized by religious hierarchies are present across most religious denominations, and there are also various monastic retreat settings available for visitors to stay in. Although the duration, purpose, and style of retreats vary, the occasion provides clergy with the chance to get away, rest from having to direct their attention to problems, not worry about physical needs, and receive support or spiritual input (Gill et al., 2018).

When pastors experience emotional exhaustion during burnout, it may also be a result of the ways pastors are inundated with those who need their attention in the areas of advisement, funerals, pre- and post-ministry, and counseling. Pastors may go through periods of emotional exhaustion when they have numerous administrative demands, are counseling members, and must attend to other obligations (Whiting, 2017). Emotional exhaustion consists of feelings of being emotionally overextended and exhausted by one's work. An individual experiencing exhaustion may feel drained lacking in energy, making them unable to unwind or recover (Dunbar et al., 2018).

Pastors may experience emotional exhaustion for many reasons, and this results in the need to rejuvenate. The job of a pastor is never finished, since they face a continuous barrage of services, weddings, funerals, meetings, crises, and conflicts. They have shut-ins to visit, sick people to see, and administrative tasks to accomplish. These responsibilities can easily result in pastors working long hours, skipping days off, and cutting their vacations short (Ream, 2016). Some pastors feel the need to be present to handle members' conflicts and experiences.

A way to potentially address burnout is for pastors to take time and space away from their responsibilities. Rest-taking may include an extended time away from the regular routine of ministry in the form of a vacation or a sabbatical. To aid pastors in coping with emotional exhaustion during burnout, they can seek resources such as trusted denominational leaders, ministerial materials, resiliency materials, mental health resources, and counseling retreats. Scholarly reading, mentorship, independent Bible study, retreats, and time out with family can also be supportive factors when integrated into their regimen. Clergy peer groups serve different purposes but are useful options. Some provide clergy safe places to express feelings, experience accountability, test ideas, and, in some cases, prepare themselves for different ministries.

Depersonalization

People may fall into the second stage of burnout, known as depersonalization, in which one chooses to distance themselves mentally and emotionally from others when they feel frustration and fatigue. The term depersonalization is categorized as detachment from others who need help, treatment, or training. It is a cynical answer to the disconnection with customers or patients who may strain the provider who is suffering from burnout. Pastors encounter adverse effects when boundaries are not well-formed or kept between their individual and occupational lives (Frederick et al., 2018). Sarcasm, thoughtlessness, and cynical attitudes toward church members may emerge because of burnout in clergy members and pastors. Religious clerics rank among the most vulnerable groups to burnout (Hester, 2018).

A pastor may assume a contrary attitude when working with church members, other leaders in the church or denominational authority (Lewis, 2017). They can appear to air their concerns and issues across the pulpit during announcements or sermons without realizing how they are coming across to their congregation. Depersonalization is the way a person creates negative views of others in their own minds. It is a minimizing of the humanity of the other, and the other becomes an entity instead of an individual. In other words, in the caregiver's eyes, the other person becomes the cause of their burnout. When a pastor loses the desire for the needed ministry duties of preaching and leading, it indicates that the pastor is waning (Gildner, 2016).

If pastors experience depersonalization, this could mean that they are tremendously inundated with leading and responding to the needs of their parishioners, their communities, and their personal family units. They may do so to the extent that they become overwhelmed. Feeling overwhelmed and exhausted leads to attempts to distance oneself emotionally and cognitively from the demands of the job. This can in turn lead to depersonalization, cynical attitudes toward clients, patients, students, or in the case of religious clergy, parishioners and staff.

Pastors experience depersonalization when their views of those they lead become negatively focused. Depersonalization is a change in how one views others. It is a minimizing of the humanity of the other, as the other becomes an object instead of a person. In the worst-case scenario, the other is seen as the cause of the burnout.

Individuals may encounter depersonalization, the second dimension of burnout, as a way of distancing themselves from disappointment and exhaustion (Frederick et al., 2018). Personal stressors pastors experience can contribute to their not fully caring or engaging enough. Going through personal struggles, such as issues with children or spouses, contributes to this. It is unfortunate that some who experience issues with their children struggle with the need to balance their families and ministries. Those who struggle with their spouses in divorce or separation are often led to burnout. Unlike other professions, the clergy's homelife is connected with their calling (Gill et al., 2018).

Pastors who normally become emotionally detached through depersonalization can experience an unconcerned or non-caring attitude toward those they are leading in church and their communities. In other words, depersonalization is a defensive response to, or disengagement with, the clients or patients who make demands on the service provider who is experiencing burnout. Pastors experience negative effects when boundaries are not well-established or maintained between their personal lives and their professional lives (Frederick et al., 2018).

Loss of Personal Achievement

Loss of personal achievement is the third stage of burnout clergy usually encounter. It is based on how the person views the goals they set out to accomplish, and their interactions with others (Frederick et al., 2018). A clergy member may experience decreased motivation to perform beyond what is expected of them due to lack of achievement. They might not be as effective as they once were, and over a process of time, they may slip into a downward spiral in job performance (Beavis, 2015). The pastor who normally struggles with personal issues, coupled with lack of support from their denomination, can succumb to burnout. Low recognition for achievements can affect a clergy member's morale to the extent of succumbing to burnout. (Williams, 2019).

A low sense of accomplishment is a form of burnout that pastors face. Burnout has a way of eradicating the triumphs and successes of clergy members to the point where they are not able to perceive reasons to commemorate success. It is unfortunate that many pastors measure their success by the number of congregants that attend their churches, or how their annual budgets either meet or exceed denominational goals. Clergy member's families and communities are also prone to experiencing burnout. Burnout negatively affects those who are close to the clergy member (Soto, 2015).

Family members, church congregations, and leaders within communities' experience indications of burnout as well. The signs that clergy members experience physically and emotionally are revealed long before the visible signs of burnout. Clergy conceal their feelings to the extent of masking the need to seek help. For clergy members to deal with burnout, they must not turn to silence while they deal with their issues internally (Soto, 2015).

Burnout is defined as a loss of efficacy and belief in work, coupled with diminished vitality, passion, and self-confidence. Willimon's (1989) observations recorded that challenging work not only reveals burnout but also comes from a lack of dedication, attention, and significance. Pastors and medical caretakers share similar experiences with burnout. Medical caretakers have the option to stop working with those they take care of, whereas pastors do not. Regardless of the personal struggle's pastors experience, usually, they do not stop working with parishioners. Maslach et al. (2001) conducted a study that emphasized the significance of church/pastoral kindness, because inappropriate interactions with church members have triggered a decrease in pastors' feelings of belonging to the congregation. As a result, it is difficult for pastors to continue working with those who have caused tension and conflict in the church. (Chen, 2020).

Marital and Family Stress

One in three pastors leave the ministry, and pastors rank third among specialists who have been divorced due to marital suffering (Lewis, 2017). When divorced clerics were questioned about the most significant problem that led to their divorce, they expressed that their work obligations were connected to their issues within the marriage and their occupation (Trihub et al., 2010). However, higher work involvement does not always produce positive organizational outcomes, because the unavoidable work-life strain on workaholics can deter their overall productivity. This imbalance of work and life makes them more likely to display petulance, negligence, and impatience (Vitello et al., 2016).

Pastors face many life challenges, but some common stressors include marital and premarital issues, fiscal management, family life, and sickness. Pastors often feel that they must be all things to all people, and that is a stressor. There are times in which the pastor must drop their current tasks to minister to the local congregation's needs. Some stressors can be the unexpected death of a parishioner, a personal emergency, a structural issue within a church building, and there are many more. These issues can divert the pastor, and this can cause stress. Pastors are expected to perform and complete a wide range of duties that contribute to feeling overworked and underpaid (Lewis, 2017).

The pastor's family can also suffer burnout because of the demands of ministry. They may fail to address their own needs, causing stress and strain on familial relationships. This is because the clergy member's life at home is directly connected with their profession (Gill et al., 2018). Family members of clergy members can understand how the church affects their family. Clergy bring home the problems from the church. (Lee, 2017). The pastor's family is involved through hearing about the stressful events that occur. The family may begin to develop negative views of parishioners and church staff members due to their clergy members' demands (Brewer et al., 2017). Clergy often do not want their church members to perceive any potential flaws or susceptibility to the point that their position within the organization is altered (Gill et al., 2018).

The clergy member's family's quality of life is affected through personal boundaries that parishioners breach. As a result, the clergy member also suffers from physical, mental, emotional, and spiritual exhaustion (Lee, 2017). The church as a workplace is structured to not be infiltrated by the lives of the clergy and their families, who bring their personal issues from home (Tanner & Zvonkovic, 2011). Parishioner invasiveness could be aggravated if the clergy member's family unit resides in a rectory, because parishioners may feel they have immediate access to the pastor. Imposition by the members of the church may cause the clergy member's family stress and interrupt their privacy. Mental imposition is worse than parishioner intrusion. The reason it is worse is because the clergy member takes to heart what they hear spoken about them from church members. (Brewer et al., 2017).

Additionally, some clergy members believe ministry to church members should come before their responsibilities at home. This leads to conflict in the clergy member's family because of the tensions between the needs of the family and the needs of the church. Managing tactics could be necessary to help clergy members and their families develop flexibility and moderate harmful results. Clergy members experience stressors such as incomplete work assignments, insufficient fiscal payments, and negative interactions between church members and the clergy member's family (Brewer et al., 2017).

Maslach (2003) posited that there is an obvious connection sandwiched between the age of a person and burnout itself. He further stated that younger people deal with more burnout than adults do. Younger clergy members are more prone to experience emotional exhaustion than older clergy members (Francis et al.,

2004). He asserted that the earlier a person is in their career, the more they experience burnout (Bassford, 2008).

Clergy often times commonly report economic stress. Clergy compensation fluctuates significantly based on the denomination, size of the congregation, and educational status of parishioners. Clergy deal with this constant stress at work. The public is aware of clergy professionals' salary, but unlike other care-based professions that receive wage increases, clergy or pastors often do not. Although economic stress is shared throughout the church, many pastors feel they should not be concerned with a rise in their salary, but with what God has called them to (Gill et al., 2018).

Pastors who begin to feel the effects of burnout can begin to lose the desire to lead and pastor with the excitement they once had, and the vision and positivity that once sparked them. While this is destructive for the individual, it also negatively impacts the pastor's family and the congregation. The cost of unhealthy and burned-out pastors is high (Hebden, 2020). Church members have elevated expectations from them, and clergy can deal with impractical anticipations to the point they feel they are constantly under a microscope (Gill et al., 2018). Developing the ability to recuperate from clergy burnout begins with recognizing what clergy burnout is. Instead of allowing burnout to be a warning of disappointment, clergy members ought to respect burnout as a cautionary defense system that alerts them when things have shifted negatively (Brewer et al., 2017).

The clergy person's family is thoroughly involved in their religious profession. Congregants expect the clergy's family to be the model family that is hospitable to everyone. But the inconsistent work schedules have made it problematic for pastors to balance family and church obligations. These families are expected to be perfect and always available to help others. Clergy are expected to be present to lead religious and worship services each weekend. They are obligated to church schedules throughout each week, leaving their families with few possibilities for family time outside the church setting (Gill et al., 2018).

Planned family events may be diverted due to the demands of the ministry. Holidays such as Christmas, Thanksgiving, and Easter frequently take a toll on clergy families due to the many worship services that the church requires. Church officials could work instead to plan a church calendar that better aligns with the pastors. (Gill et al., 2018). Some clergy struggle with boundaries between their work role and individual lives, since their duties are entangled with individual spiritual development (Heck et al., 2018).

Some challenges include sharing stress from undefined or extreme role expectations, recurrent moves for example, from district to district, state to state, or within a city or town to include church members who may intrude on the pastor's family time with their family. Additionally, clergy have identified the potential for frequent activities with sometimes little control or input as stressful. It can be difficult for family members to establish new relationships due to frequently relocating. Frequent moves can negatively impact the lives of clergy children and the spouse and their career ambitions (Snelgar et al., 2017). Geographic relocation causes anxiety and requires many changes (Lewis, 2017). It is not unusual for clergy spouses to experience emotional difficulties resulting in depression (Speight & Speight, 2017).

The grief care pastors, and clergy professionals provide for people can also lead to burnout. They counsel people but are often affected by what they hear. The chaplain can speak from the platform of grief or bereavement and how it has affected them. Anne Marie Miller in her book *Beating Burnout* illuminates the effects of burnout in ministry as a leader: stress and burnout can cause us to project our pain and exhaustion on others, usually those closest to us. Some people respond to burnout by lashing out and storming around in a rage because they feel their lives are falling apart. Exhaustion can cause us to shut down and stop communicating with our spouse or our friends. And by "communicating," I mean both talking and listening. We no longer feel connected to those around us, and we begin to not care about nurturing those relationships that God has placed in our lives. Resentment can develop after not communicating for a while. Our spouses or friends may not feel comfortable opening to us anymore, and bitterness can be formed and directed toward us, toward the church, and even toward God (Miller, 2014).

Resentment can ensue with family members due to ministry demands on their loved ones. It invariably causes conflict in the family, thereby perpetuating potential misunderstandings among family members and division in the home. The result is conflict in the clergy family due to the tension between family needs and ministry demands. Coping strategies are needed to assist clergy and their families in developing resilience and mitigating the negative effects of demands and stressors such as heavy workloads, inadequate financial compensation, and boundary ambiguity between the congregation and the clergy's family (Brewer et al., 2017).

I noted stressors such as the need for pastors to be available 24/7, and what happens when boundaries are breached during burnout. The pastors' experiences during the burnout stage, along with that of their family members, are where a pastor always working. Results from qualitative interviews proved that some of the pastors interviewed suffered from frustration, mental fatigue, emotional detachment, and being overwhelmed. It was also discovered that a resource for pastors during burnout is other pastors, along with books and periodicals. Clergy work every weekend and have frequent commitments with church activities, often at night and outside normal working hours, thus leaving the clergy family with few options for social outlets outside of the church (Gill et al., 2018).

At the same time, clergy family events can often be interrupted or affected by the demands of ministry. From the literature review, special occasions like Christmas and Easter are seen as fun family holidays, but they can be stressful times for clergy and their family, as additional worship services are held and tasks multiply. Thus, it can be difficult for clergy to find space and time for experiences that do not drain their attention or resources (Gill et al., 2018). The job of a pastor is more of a lifestyle, and it involves the whole family. Pastors spend much of their work time investing in others, sometimes at the deficit of caring for themselves or investing their time well at home (Burnette, 2016). The pastor's family may not be able to get a break with their family members. Evidence specifies that the elevated expectations placed on their time were among the main reasons clergy go through burnout (Jackson-Jordan, 2013).

Chronic Stress and Inadequate Rest

Ministry difficulties and their distinctive attributes lead to tension and burnout, and at times end in clergy deciding to switch vocations, abandoning church ministry entirely (Tanner & Zvonkovic, 2011). Over time, increased blood pressure and heart rate can facilitate a predisposition to heart attacks and strokes. Mental health issues from chronic stress comprise depression and anxiety. Therefore, chronic stress in clergy creates personal health risks and encroaches destructively on their relationships with family members and congregations (Heck et al., 2017). Outcomes of chronic stress include sleep deprivation, sickness, irritability, increased blood pressure, raised heart rate, inflammation, unwillingness of the immune system, and appetite disruption (Heck et al., 2017).

Rest is viewed as either a remedy for burnout or a preemptive gauge against it. Rest is commonly recommended for high-stress occupations such as charity workers, missionaries, and clergy members. A Sabbath rest, as many religions call it, can be a healthy practice for pastors. Sabbath rest is a preemptive method for burnout and is a healthful tradition—an enrichment of a person's spiritual vitality (White et al., 2015). Resting well means disconnecting oneself from responsibilities and going out of town or away from church issues. Clergy work weekends, which means that they need to dedicate time to rest from regular church obligations and activities. (Gill et al., 2018).

Clergy can collapse due to improper respite. Many pastors view time off as "an act of truancy" (Brewer, 2016, p. 51). Rest should be a priority within pastors' schedules and not viewed as a waste of their time (Brewer, 2016). Pastors can experience a variety of sickness resulting from burnout and turmoil. Prioritizing taking time to rest will help combat the decline of their emotional, mental, spiritual, and physical assets.

Rest can be circumstantially associated with helping avert

exhaustion and increasing pliability (Brewer, 2016). Clergy members need to take a day off at least once a week. As they do this, they should delegate their responsibilities beforehand to those who are trusted to lead the church organization in their absence while mustering up the courage to say no when they should. Vacation should be a time of intentionality to rest and recuperate but not forgetting to educate oneself with new and innovative knowledge (Brewer, 2016).

Being On-Call 24/7

The 24/7 mentality expects pastors to provide ministry to those they lead in the church setting 24/7. Pastoral ministry and the responsibilities that come with it can lead to burnout. Interacting with parishioners by helping them deal with their spiritual and personal issues can be taxing for the pastor (Strong, 2017). Pastors offer ministry in emergency visitations in homes and hospitals, interception of marital conflicts, last rites, baby dedications, counseling, and even bailing people out of jail. This can create unhealthy boundaries for both the church and the clergy who serve as pastors, because church members always desire and expect the accessibility of the pastor.

The pastor is viewed as the iconoclastic father or mother figurehead of the local church by many church members. The result of this view is pastors who strive to fulfill the impractical expectations of all church members. Excessive workloads, not requesting help when they need it, and making themselves available to church members may cause the pastor to burn out. Clergy who serve in pastoral roles need to be replenished spiritually and mentally after they pour themselves into those in need of their help (Muse et al., 2016). Evidence specifies that elevated expectations for their time were among the main reasons clergy go through burnout (Jackson-Jordan, 2013). The pastor's job encompasses the whole family. Pastors spend a lot of their time at work taking care of parishioners, sometimes at the shortfall of taking care of themselves and supporting their families (Burnette, 2016).

Pastoral ministers in African American communities, who may serve in troubled, neglected inner-city neighborhoods, often experience extreme stress dealing with the overwhelming number of crises, violence, abuse, and disruption that confront their congregants and community. Black preachers have an extensive history of serving others and leading human rights movements. In fact, it started when they spoke out about the institution of slavery from their church pulpits. These pastors would lead movements and later form alliances with leaders of communities, pertaining to its Black citizens and the troubles they still face today of unfair treatment, inadequate living conditions, and low wages. (Joiner, 2020).

As the central figure of the church, and often the only "glue" holding a group of people together, the pastor takes on numerous leadership roles for which they are not properly prepared, which often leads to burnout. Schools and seminaries within the United States do not properly prepare their ministers to serve churches in the twenty-first century. Pastors and ministers of churches are positioned to lead churches with high mandates from denominational and independent churches and elevated expectations (Exantus, 2011). Stress and burnout can accumulate from the pressure to "be there for others," to excel at their job, and to exhibit honesty at all times despite complex environments.

CHAPTER TWO

Behavioral Signs the Pastor Experiences "I'm Good!"

Behavioral Signs of Pastoral Burnout

There can be many behavioral signs of pastoral burnout. Some pastors may lead by instilling fear, thereby causing morale to suffer. Employees of the church can become withdrawn, frightened, insulted, and damaged when the pastor leads in a toxic manner (Harper & Reynolds, 2017). Pastors may find it challenging to delegate responsibilities to other staff or ministry leaders of a church.

Some pastors find it difficult to let go of responsibilities because they feel that the duties must be accomplished. Staff and ministry leaders can view the pastor as responsible for controlling job tasks. Garnering the ability to trust those they lead will reduce the pastor's workload, thereby enabling them to focus on other needed items in the church setting. Yet, callous, rude, and corrupt pastoral leaders can be a problem in the workplace. Followers of an organization will lose trust in those who lead in a toxic manner (Harper & Reynolds, 2017).

Within the religious hierarchical infrastructures of church administration, various pastors battle with loneliness during burnout. When pastors serve under the oversight of senior denominational leaders without social interaction, they can find themselves feeling lonely. Loneliness sets in when few people understand the role and strains of the pastor (Lewis, 2017).

Clergy members who endure burnout have ways of surviving when they are dealing with loneliness. The most important aspect of handling burnout is that one must confront oneself. This requires a precise and candid examination of one's solitude and then a rediscovery of connections with acquaintances or colleagues (Rokach, 2018). Clergy members and pastors suffer from loneliness as they try to take on their vast workloads with little time and supplies. Being isolated and having extreme work overload has ties to burnout among pastors and clergy professionals (Miner et al., 2010).

Pastors who serve small churches by themselves, without other church ministerial support, spend a lot of their week ensuring they provide pastoral oversight and care for the congregants. The lone pastor is expected to do it all. This same person is expected to be the futurist who is a magnificent orator. The pastor is expected to effectively teach spiritual disciplines, serve as the educator of religion, serve as the youth pastor, serve as the deacon, serve as the usher, and serve as the musician who is acquainted with the musical needs the of the congregation Pastors are also expected to grow the church exponentially. In addition, they are expected to visit the sick, perform nursing home visits, perform jail visits, provide premarital and marital counseling, and other requested functions (Only, 2021).

Pastors in rural areas experience loneliness as serving as the only minister of the local church. Rural churches usually operate under the leadership of a single pastor who divides their time between congregations as needed. The rural pastor must manage the organization by themselves, and this includes sermon preparation for weekly worship services, financial development, management of the church office, and nurturing and tending to the church members' individual spiritual needs (Lovell & Scott, 2015). Pastors who serve small churches are more susceptible to burnout than pastors of large churches. The reason for this is that smaller churches have more interpersonal relationships than larger churches. Burnout is the cause of attrition in smaller churches, it is important to ascertain the reasons why (White, 2020).

Emotional Health and Wellbeing

Previous research has examined clergy members' natural and mental wellbeing. However, previous research has disregarded ministerial interest. Clergy members are susceptible to mental fatigue and trouble with focus. Some of the symptoms include being unable to focus or cope with interruptions, make choices, or resolve difficulties. Mental fatigue can be conquered along with analytical capability being reestablished by visiting peaceful environments that allow fixed attention to rest (Gill et al., 2018).

Clergy experience continuous pressures and frequent strains, which empty their mental capacities and lessen their ability to concentrate. However, clergy need to maintain attention to be able to assist their parishioners. They must be intentional in their availability to help parishioners listen and solve problems, provide wisdom, and avoid distractions of their own. These steps are crucial for the personal welfare of clergy and the maintenance of the relationships with church members (Gill et al., 2018). Clergy often feel they are closely examined or disparaged for how they devote their time, chiefly if church parishioners require them to be accessible in the church office, even though much of the pastoral care tasks may be done in members' homes and medical facilities. Effects of criticism from church members can be exhausting and discouraging. Critique and tension between clergy and the church members can have a destructive effect on the clergy member's health, lifestyle, and ministerial gratification (Gill et al., 2018).

Self-Inspiration, Anxiety, Depression, and Workplace Grief

Clergy members are expected to meet the needs of those they serve in the local church. Some clergy burn out from their service to the church, but many experience burnout and never return to the church to serve in the pulpit. It does not matter how well a pastor serves and how successful they are in leading a church; they can still become tired and experience burnout (Burks, 2018). Critical church members and lack of social support are forecasters of clergy apprehension and sadness (Gill et al., 2018).

Self-inspiration may help clergy with hopelessness. Self-inspiration is a fundamental skill that provides a person with the capability to deal with difficult circumstances. Self-inspiration is also an instrument for handling stress and allowing a person to deal with anxiety, depression, and workplace grief. Research has shown that self-inspiration has a positive effect on thoughts of welfare, self-acknowledgment, and self-esteem. Self-inspiration can be a solid indicator of hope when challenging circumstances or feelings of apprehension and powerlessness arise (Williams, 2019).

Nearly all clergy mourn the loss of their church members when there is a death in the community. Unsettled workplace grief has been shown to affect happiness and physical health in various professions, including the military, nursing, and medicine. A pastor who must close a church may experience stress related to grief and stigma, resulting in shame. Pastors can experience sources of stress suffered by people in other professions and careers. Receiving respect from parishioners and denominational hierarchies may mean more to a pastor than to someone with a different domain.

Pastors have what has been called a profoundly structured, specialized individuality that shapes their occupation. Being a pastor involves a commitment to pastoral oaths and God (Cafferata, 2017).

Hardships in pastoral leadership in the United States are being researched especially with churches that require much of pastors who serve them. This can also include those who choose to retire from the pastorate. In order for pastors to mentally survive, they must become resilient to deal with the struggles of those they pastor.

Compassion Fatigue

"Compassion fatigue" affects those who work with others and provide care for them through challenging or traumatic experiences (Scott & Lovell, 2015). Clergy often serve in various roles and responsibilities, comprised of counseling, case supervision, and understanding people in conditions that can be exceedingly repetitive. Churches play a significant part in their members' lives and church members are some of the most prone in society to suffer compassion fatigue. Clergy members are at the center of this effort, which requires sympathy and care, often underneath disconcerting conditions (Hanley, 2019).

Compassion fatigue, similar to burnout, can constrain a person's ability to preserve clear personal and professional limitations. A person who has psychological burnout can also have compassion fatigue. People who suffer and deal with compassion fatigue may find themselves experiencing the mental trauma that can come from demonstrating care for those who need their help. Compassion fatigue is also connected to diminished amounts of self-effectiveness and self-assurance, which may have damaging effects on presentation (Snelgar et al., 2017).

Compassion fatigue should be distinguished from burnout and secondary trauma, which occurs on behalf of another individual. It comprises more than inner reduction and emotional fatigue. Compassion fatigue involves spiritual fatigue and its link to worn-out hope. It is an unsuitable doctrinal frame of reference; it is about a kind of customary salutation of personal restriction and powerlessness within the sphere of responsibility, purpose, and benevolence (Louw, 2015).

Most people with compassion fatigue struggle with comparison, contrast, and illogicality while aware of these emotions. A sensible resolution involving sorrow still does not alleviate compassion fatigue from what the victim is currently experiencing. The fatigue happens because caring professionals are often subjected to the discomfort of heartbreak and irretrievable defeat. Some of the ways that caregivers reactivate themselves can include a good diet, exercise, rest, some form of meditation, the nurturing of associations outside of the work setting, and thoughtfulness toward others (Streets, 2015).

Carla Joinson, in the article *Coping with Compassion Fatigue,* alludes that nurses become compassionately attached to their patients as a part of their duty. Joinson writes about empathy and compassion as caregivers suffer it. The caregiver's feelings of sorrow and empathy was the focus of the cost of caring and the overall effects connected with it. Compassion fatigue has now been launched as a term to define the cumulative effects of the cost of caring (Joinson, 1992).

Maryann Abendroth, in her article *Overview and Summary: Compassion Fatigue: Caregivers at Risk,* does extensive research and expounds on how caregivers take compassion fatigue with them throughout their lives. Caregivers with compassion fatigue may develop a preoccupation with their patients by reexperiencing their trauma; they can develop signs of anxiety as a result of this secondary trauma. Examples of this can include difficulty falling or staying asleep, irritability or outbursts of anger, and/or exaggerated startle responses. Most importantly, these caregivers ultimately experience a reduced capacity for, or interest in, being empathic toward the suffering of others. Scholars differ in their perspectives of CF especially as it relates to burnout. However, they tend to agree that in general, CF has a more sudden and acute onset than burnout, a condition that gradually wears down caregivers who are overwhelmed and unable to effect positive change. Understanding CF can empower nurses to utilize preventive measures that promote self-care, improve patient outcomes, and optimize therapeutic relationships (Abendroth, 2011).

The pastor, clergy professional, chaplain, and other ministry leaders can indeed suffer from compassion fatigue. It is always wise to take a day off from ministry and totally detach. This is not easy for many to do as they can immerse themselves in work matters. Having experienced compassion fatigue in civilian and military ministry while in deployed and stateside settings, after hours of listening to counselees pour their hearts out, need to detox or refresh ourselves. Military chaplains must do something to relax or otherwise get the help they need so they are apt to perform and function in the military role they are appointed to. On a day-to-day basis, military chaplains immerse themselves in the lives of those who come for counsel, as suggested by Jeni Tyson.

The term "compassion fatigue" conveys the impact of empathic immersion in another human being's suffering, without pathologizing the clinician. Therefore, the term "compassion fatigue" is utilized in this paper to discuss the effects of working with combat-related trauma. Clinicians affected by compassion fatigue can experience symptoms which may parallel their client's diagnosis of post-traumatic stress disorder (PTSD) (e.g. re-experiencing the traumatic event, avoidance, psychic numbing, and hyperarousal), as defined by the Diagnostic Statistical Manual of Mental Disorders (DSM-IV) (APA, 1994) (Tyson, 2007).

Compassion fatigue results from working with and listening to people that come for advice in coping with their conditions and dealing with problems back home at the same time. Without realizing it, a caregiver can transmit compassion fatigue to members of their family through anger, words of hurt, and depression. Those who suffer from compassion fatigue suffer because they care about the people who come to them with their struggles.

Charles Figley gives reasons why the counselee and counselor have an alliance in therapy. Some would argue that it is wrong for a practitioner to have deep feelings of sympathy and sorrow for their client's suffering. Yet systematic studies of the efficacy of therapy point to the therapeutic alliance between client and clinician— the ability to empathize, to understand and help clients. If absent, therapeutic progress is highly unlikely. The most important ingredients in building therapeutic alliances include the client liking and trusting their therapist. And these feelings are directly related to the degree to which the therapist utilizes and expresses empathy and compassion.

Della Stewart, in her article *Compassion Fatigue: What Is the Level Among Army Chaplains,* includes thorough research about compassion fatigue. Compassion fatigue is gradual and can take years to develop. Symptoms include intrusive thoughts, sleep disturbances, anxiety, and loss of hope. Contributing factors are age, lack of job experience, history of previous trauma, lack of support, repetitive exposure to trauma victims, high clinical caseloads of trauma survivors, codependency relative to those being counseled, multiple patients dying within a short period of time, and lack of balance between work, rest, and play (Stewart 2012).

Compassion fatigue for the sufferer is also a form of burnout. Stewart further defines burnout as a form of compassion fatigue. It occurs as a result of "taking care of others" rather than exposure to the traumatic events of others. Anyone dissatisfied in the workplace and constantly subjected to job stressors can experience burnout. Symptoms include withdrawal, work apathy, decline in productivity, absenteeism, and interpersonal difficulties. Burnout, unlike compassion fatigue, can be remedied by time off or a change in employment (Kalish, 1981). The caregiver or ministry professional can suffer from compassion fatigue, as they can become overwhelmed mentally and emotionally as they listen to the traumatic events the counselee has shared with them.

CHAPTER THREE

The Pastor's Experiences During Burnout

"I Feel Fine!"

Pastor's Experiences During the Burnout Phase

Pastors experience many emotional and physical changes during burnout. The journey can be complicated by poor dietary habits, lack of sleep, lack of proper exercise, or lack of recreation. The need for self-care should be the main priority in the pastor's life. Inconsistent sleep practices, senseless hours of work, strenuous physical activity, and unhealthy eating habits can all create greater problems for pastors. (Tan & Castillo, 2014). Pastors in North American experience burnout at alarming rates. Their spiritual, mental, physical, and social health is deteriorating. Clergy should employ more strategies in taking care of themselves to help them deal with burnout (Tan, & Castillo, 2014). When a person is subjected to repeated anxiety during a workday, it could worsen health conditions. A person cannot take a meaningful break while working.

People enter church ministry because they trust they can be of service to a local church. Their goal is to lead and teach parishioners to live a committed life holy to God. Clergy members experience burnout as much as other professionals do. Burnout describes a person's state in which they display low energy, low interest, and a sense of obligation (Barnard & Curry, 2012). Churches that are being led by pastors with high levels of stress also succumb to varied levels of burnout. The pastors may serve with a lack of empathy for their congregation and are not tuned into the emotions of parishioners (Brewer, 2016).

As parishioners raise their requirements and strengthen their anticipations, clergy members may decide to end their pastorate and ultimately leave the ministry (Soto, 2015). Pastors deal with natural deviations well before they show visible indications of burnout. Pastors often believe they should conceal what they feel and wear a façade. Pastors can suppress how they feel without realizing they are prolonging their burnout (Barnard & Curry, 2012).

How Pastors Lead During the Burnout Phase

Ministers who possess high degrees of compassion for others describe amplified levels of job gratification and only minor amounts of burnout while dealing with numerous stressors (Barnard & Curry, 2012). They understand that they are not alone and are better capable of staying linked with God and others through collaboration instead of attempting to navigate challenges without help. The clergy member's family is therapeutic for loneliness and lessens the pressures of church work, despite different family needs (Muse et al., 2016).

To add to the challenges, there is also the handling of conflict within the congregation. Clergy members discuss the competition amongst church members and take a leadership role while making the necessary and appropriate decisions. Sometimes these choices do not have apparent correct or incorrect responses, and clergy members become susceptible to censure in terms of limitations set by senior clergy leaders in denominations in the area of leading and preaching (Adams et al., 2016). To avoid conflict with parishioners, the pastor will seek to please the congregants (Clunan, 2016).

Leadership in congregations carries with it the added test: the leader must often rely on coaxing, trust, and the work of volunteers to get tasks done. The clergy member's spouse and children are often caught in the middle of issues they have with church members. These adverse situations can arise due to factors involving church leaders, church members, problems within the community, and church and denominational hierarchies. Utilizing attentive care is vital to answering appropriately and dealing with adverse situations within church membership (Gill et al., 2018).

How Pastors Cope During the Burnout Phase

Many pastors realize that today's ministry setting is an environment that is prone to highly stressful situations. Some ministers who have experienced pastoral burnout believe today's setting is more stressful than that of the early church leaders in the Bible (Millikin, 2018). Pastors are expected to interact interpersonally with parishioners, thereby heightening the causal effects of burnout. Burnout is experienced with those who serve in occupations where the demands are higher than the actual resources. Stressful jobs are often those where individuals feel emotional exhaustion (Rosales, 2019).

Pastors and clergy utilize approaches for surviving with ministry anxiety which includes pastimes, religious growth, different sporting activities, and time away (Anderson, 2011). When a person copes from an external source of stress, they internalize what they deal with through their emotions. Indirect coping is a strategy applied internally to one's behaviors and emotions. (Koo, 2017). Coping, in some cases, does not reduce loads of stress but increases them. (Hoover, 2021). The demonstrated need for retreats, vacations, and opportunities to attend denominational conferences are ways churches can support the pastors who serve them (Coates, 2019).

Non-monetary support of clergy members is a way of supporting pastors, which in turn averts burnout. (Coates, 2019). Vacations are ways a clergy member can rest. However, finding the time to get away from the anxieties of work can be perplexing. The time the clergy member gets away might not be sufficient in opportunities to find relaxation. Relaxation is often viewed as either a therapy for burnout or a preemptive measure counter to it. Relaxation is highly recommended for those in high strain circumstances, such as philanthropic employees, spiritual leaders, and clergy members as an everyday approach to dealing with burnout (White et al., 2015).

Pastors often make decisions about how they govern their schedules and duties that they have. The liberty they have, coupled with the establishment of sensitive and clerical requirements, permits pastors to make use of a variety of actions to manage job pressure.

Academic study, meetings, counseling, preaching, teaching, mentoring, Bible studies, denominational conferences, and family time could be incorporated into a daily routine. Most Pastors often have independence with significant leeway in their daily and weekly schedules. The liberty, coupled with surrounding expressive and organizational strains, allows clergy to gauge numerous actions to manage occupational stress. The acquiring of educational materials, receiving mentorship, interacting in Bible study, attending retreats, and spending time with family can all be incorporated into their routine.

Clergy often cope by meeting with their peers. As they seek and make the efforts to meet with peers, it helps them understand they are not alone. Peer groups can also provide various purposes for clergy members. Some groups provide clergy members safe places for being true to who they are, experiencing spiritual growth, sharing ideas, and, in many instances, to preparing for new ministry opportunities. Clergy peer groups address some of the concerns about clergy tension they face (Sixbey, 2014). These groups serve as an instrument for the pastor to cope with the daily or weekly pressures of ministry.

Taking time to walk in natural settings, if possible, and also engaging with the atmosphere can be highly advantageous for mental rejuvenation (Gill et al., 2018). Pastors must take time away from work to rest and recuperate. Pastors who support their denomination's leaders in promoting spiritual and mental wellness are vital to leadership and service. For pastors to take time away from work for rest and recovery without denominational opposition promotes a healthy work ethic for pastoral leaders. Local pastors may promote the same attitude with their church staff by encouraging their staff members to take time away from work to rest and recuperate (Hough, 2019).

Leaders of denominations desire clergy members to maintain consistently healthy spiritual and mental health to be fully present for their congregations (Hough, 2019). The blessing of experiencing spiritual refreshment for a pastor is much needed to ensure their spiritual vitality as they lead their families and congregations. Yearly religious retreats organized by denominational leaders are customary throughout the country, and there are also various reclusive haven locations. While the period, reason, and aim of retreats differ, the time delivers the opportunity for clergy to be absent from work, rest, and relieve themselves of their obligations to their congregations while receiving spiritual edification (Gill et al., 2018).

CHAPTER FOUR

The Pastor and Bereavement Ministry "I Don't Know…"

Bereavement Ministry

Bereavement, or "grief ministry" as some refer to it, is a wonderful ministry to serve in. One must certainly know they are called to serve in it or else they may burn out very quickly. In giving oneself to helping others cope with grief and loss, the pastor or clergy member who serves in this ministry must be able to detach themselves emotionally from those who are grieving. That may sound harsh or uncaring, but it is not. The transfer of emotions from those who are hurting in general, let alone those who are grieving, can weigh down on a person so much so that one can be affected physically and mentally.

I can never forget, in late spring of 2013, in one week, our military base experienced two deaths of military officers; one committed suicide and the other died from a motorcycle accident. It was a very tedious and mentally tiring/sickening task afterward to provide ministry not only to their families, but also to their units. Both funerals totaled over three hundred in attendance. I had to pray on my way home for strength as I attempted to drive home after the second funeral. I did not realize how grief had overtaken me as I arrived in my driveway; I could not open my car door.

When I arrived home, I could not understand why I had had trouble with getting out of my car. As I opened my car door and began to get out of my car, I fell to the ground. One of my family members came out of the house and picked me up, but then I collapsed, not realizing the emotional, or rather mental, pain that I was in. It was at the point that it made me physically sick for a few days, and I had to take time off work.

Some weeks afterward, the last individuals of the two late military officers' units concluded bereavement counseling with me and a couple of other chaplains in our base chapel. I still receive calls from their families, not as frequently as I used to, but the main question I am asked is "Why?" The military chaplain cannot always answer this question. All we can do is listen as they recount a multitude of events leading up to the death of their loved one. No matter how tiring it may seem, the counselee who is bereaved needs to go through catharsis by expressing their feelings and thoughts verbally to the chaplain. It helps in the coping process and in accepting what happened.

Bill Flatt wrote how those who grieve should be allowed to express themselves. Expressing your thoughts and feelings openly, talking them out and crying if you feel like it, is one of the best things you can do to deal with your grief. Keeping it all bottled up inside just isn't healthy and makes the grieving process last longer than it otherwise would. Talking to someone else during your grieving helps first just because it gives you an outlet for your strong feelings. It's only natural to want to talk about something that's so important to you, and it's frustrating when you don't have an opportunity to do so (Flatt, 1987).

Besides that, it's just easier to get through any difficult time or experience if you know someone else is going through it with you, shoulder to shoulder. As the Bible says in Proverbs 27:17: "Iron sharpens iron; so, a man sharpens the countenance of his friend." Talking about your feelings will help you sort through them, get a little more perspective, and perhaps gain some insight into them. Have you ever noticed how you can get an idea about something, and then as you begin to talk to a friend about it, different aspects of it or a different perspective on it will emerge? The person listening to you doesn't need to say much, if anything, either. Your own words trigger your thought processes.

It is therapeutic to allow the grieving to express their feelings. The grieving must be allowed to cry out, allowed to let the tears to flow, and allowed to scream if needed, which is why I agree with the author. These expressions allow the person to begin to heal emotionally. The grieving person being allowed to grieve verbally is my primary reason for agreeing with the author. Helen Harris imparts in her book, *What Is a Congregation to Do? Grief in Family Congregational Life,* how a congregation can go above and beyond by serving a grieving family within their congregation:

1. Be present. Be a part of the rescue team, bring meals, start a prayer chain, care for the surviving child, meet financial needs for hospital and funeral costs, sit in the emergency room and the intensive care waiting room. Keep being present a year after the death and even ten and twenty years after the death.

2. Listen to the story as many times as the bereaved need to tell it. The key to being helpful is hearing the story every time as though it were the first. Those in crisis and those who have lost someone important to them have to find a way to make sense of the experience. Telling it to a good listener is the most effective intervention.

3. Be honest. Provide information that is accurate and simple in small increments. It is not necessary to tell all truth at once. Persons in crisis need time to absorb the realities of death and loss.

4. Never take away hope. Persons in crisis deal with reality as they are ready. Being honest does not mean communicating hopelessness. Allow people to reframe their hope as they are ready. A mother once expressed hope that she would be healed, then that she wouldn't hurt, and finally that her children would be cared for after she was gone. She was never without hope. The content and focus of her hope just changed over time.

5. Be available over time. The process of grief takes years. The entire first year after a loss is one struggle after another. Mark your calendar and send a note or call on special occasions like birthdays, anniversaries, holidays, and the anniversary of the death. Remember that the bereaved might be thinking about when their child would have graduated from high school, mourning the secondary loss of the grandchildren they will never have, and they will continue to deal with these losses over time.

6. Don't box people into artificial stages or categories. Normalize the grief experience with language of feelings and permission to experience those feelings. Don't tell people what they must or must not do. Each person must find the expressions of grief that are helpful to them and those that are not.

7. Provide spiritual support by allowing people to live the questions. God can handle expressions of anger or questions. Let the belief system of the bereaved guide discussions about life after death, the sources of hope for the future. Be the presence of God when the bereaved cannot see or feel God.

8. Speak the name of the deceased. It is helpful to provide rituals of remembering that honor the deceased. A great fear of the bereaved is that their loved one will not be remembered. Ask how the deceased can be remembered for years after the loss.

9. Remember that people who are grieving are not locked in time. They age, grow, change, and enter new life stages as well. Allow the normative changes of life without judgment. A bereaved husband may, with time, marry again. A dying teenager once shared with me his prayer that his parents would have another child soon, not to replace him, but because they were such incredible parents. As the bereaved begin new stages of their lives, they will continue to remember all the relationships that were lost.

10. Offer readings on grief to the bereaved, understanding that the ability to accept them and with what timing will vary from person to person.

11. Trust your own intuitive awareness. What you say is less important than you being there. Take care of yourself so that you can care for others. Model self-care.

In an era of families often stretched across great geographic distances, congregations are in a unique position to offer family to those who are isolated by grief or distance or both. The love and nurturing that are naturally part of the spiritual family experience are the foundational pieces of congregations reaching out to those who are grieving.

The advice given by Helen Harris gives clarity and understanding that translates to my learning to effectively serve as a pastor when it comes to grief. I agree with Helen Harris in all eleven points she wrote in her article. However, I agree most of all with the last point in that the caregiver must take care of themselves. I believe the person giving care to others cannot effectively give that care unless they allow themselves to relax and rest from giving bereavement care.

Vicarious Traumatization

Vicarious traumatization is another cause of burnout among pastors and clergy personnel. Witnessing events that stick in your head for a prolonged period affects you as witnessing the death of a person, or a loved one does. The term "vicarious traumatization" means "the phenomena of transmission of traumatic stress by bearing witness to the stories of traumatic events."21 This is a very similar term to compassion fatigue. However, Saakvitne and Pearlman further describe vicarious traumatization as "the transformation of the therapist's or helper's inner experience as a result of empathic engagement with survivor clients and their trauma material. Simply put, when we open our hearts to hear someone's story of devastation or betrayal, our cherished beliefs are challenged, and we are changed."

Vicarious traumatization is also the stress that is transmitted to individuals through hearing about the trauma by nature of a personal or professional relationship and the empathic ability present in the listener. Often this is the case in the deployed setting and sometimes in the stateside setting as well. When the stressor or the possibility of war is imminent, and one must also hear from the counselee and the stressors of their lives, vicarious traumatization takes effect in the counselor or caring professional.

Vicarious traumatic reactions involve profound changes in the schema and core aspect of the counselor's self. These reactions involve changes in the counselor's identity, beliefs, and memory (Pearlman and Saakvitne, 1996). Jan Nelson and David Eaker conduct extensive research and address the importance of setting up a program of bereavement care after a traumatic event.

The phases of grieving after such traumatic events are similar to the phases of grieving after someone has died. In some of these catastrophes, people may have seen family members, neighbors, friends, and even strangers die before their eyes.

They may have tried to rescue them but were unable to do so.

As people deal with severe trauma, many people will regress back to previous ways of coping. They may start smoking, drinking, or taking drugs again (Nelson & Eaker, 1988).

Even though regression is natural to the grieving process, alcohol and drugs can inhibit progress through the grief cycle and prevent the bereaved from doing the difficult work required. Try to work with them early on, especially if you are knowledgeable of past behaviors. Each kind of trauma creates unique pain and unique challenges. Remember that individuals can respond differently; there isn't a wrong way to grieve. Attitudes such as self-blame, guilt, blaming others, and extreme anger, are part of the normal process of grieving, but they need to be addressed so that those grieving are able to resolve them. Remember: these attitudes, thoughts, feelings, and behaviors are normal responses to abnormal situations (Nelson and Eaker, 1988).

7 Stages of Grief

1. **Shock and Denial**: A person will react to learning of the loss; denying reality.

2. **Pain & Guilt**: As the shock wears off, it is replaced with the unbelievable pain.

3. **Anger and Bargaining**: A person may lash out and lay blame for the death on someone else.

4. **Depression, Reflection, Loneliness**: It needs to take its course, "no talking out of it;" reality.

5. **The Upward Turn**: As they begin to adjust their life, calmness ensues; depression lightens.

6. **Reconstruction and Work-Through**: A person becomes more functional without the deceased.

7. **Acceptance and Hope**: A person accepts reality, finds a way forward, has hope for living.

Grief Work

You as a pastor or ministry professional can burn out if you do not allow yourself to be the listener. When a person is grieving, they do not need a lot of scriptures quoted to them. Your job as the ministerial professional is to be the listening. Being the listener and being present are your greatest ministries to a person or a family.

A person can experience grief for a lifetime. Most learn to live and grow with it after they have accepted the loss, which is the last step in the grieving process. This depends on how close the person was with the deceased. It may take quite some time for things to get back to some sense of normalcy. The path to normalcy is called "grief work," which is a person learning over time to emancipate themselves from the deceased.

In other words, as they grow through grief, healing takes place in terms of crying, if need be, undergoing therapeutic counseling, and "talking it out" repeatedly, which facilitates healing for the grieving person. Feelings of grief are normal. Crying is healing, anger is natural, and expressing one's feelings is needed as that person grieves. Sharing our tears with our significant others brings about healing and understanding over time.

For example, if a husband and wife lose a child, both parents need to express their grief openly and to one another, in front of the other children and friends. It is good for the man especially to share his tears with his wife and for the wife to know that her husband grieves with her. He expresses his feelings of loss through his tears. In this, there forms a fostering of healing for them both. It is not uncommon for the wife to feel that because her husband is not feeling the loss in crying and he is not crying out loud, he is not feeling the loss at all. He cries in ways she may never know about unless he reveals them in time to her.

Anticipatory Grief

As a professional, please do not allow yourself to become burnt out by those who come to you in fear, wearing you out with the inevitability of an impending death of a loved one or the death of a relationship/divorce. Take it from me; I have the experience to prove to you that you will be worn out and burnt out if you fall into this situation. Anticipatory grief is simply the expectation of the death of a loved one whether it be a short or a prolonged amount of time. It may take years for a person to heal and grow to accept that their loved one has passed away.

Depending on how close a person was to their deceased loved one is proportionate to the level of grief they will have. If a person is a distant relative of the deceased, they may not suffer with grief nowhere to the extent of a person who was closer to them in terms of relationship. The distant relative may possibly not shed a tear at the funeral or memorial service. If a person was a very close relative of the deceased, they may require intensive therapy to assist them as they heal and later accept the passing of their loved one.

When it comes to relationships, people can sense when a relationship is on the edge of its demise. They will come to you for guidance and help. As you share wisdom and pray with them, allow the Holy Spirit to lead and guide you in what to say and how to handle dealing with them. Their spirit can be vulnerable and sensitive. You, as a pastor, cannot handle them harshly. Handle them with care.

CHAPTER FIVE

The Pastor Must Learn to Become Resilient

"I Can Do This!"

Resilience

Resilience means to bounce back. Those of us who serve in facets of ministry refer to this as "a daily devotion." We all have challenges in life. There are times it seems virtually impossible to bounce back into reality from a tragic or traumatic event. Robert Wicks, the author of the book *Bounce,* visited a military installation I was once stationed at. I had the privilege and honor to sit with him for a few moments before he spoke at the base resiliency program. I asked him, "How can a military caregiver bounce back into regular life just after coming from a combat environment?" Wicks stressed to me how important it is to take time on a daily basis to be quiet.

Time spent in silence and solitude on a regular basis can affect us in a number of ways. Wicks encouraged me to read the following in his book just before the program started:

Meditation

- Sharpens our sense of clarity about the life we are living and the choices we are making.

- Enhances our attitude of simplicity.

- Increases our humility and helps us avoid unnecessary arrogance by allowing time to examine our defenses and the games we play (these often become apparent during quiet times)

- Let's us enjoy our relationship with ourselves more.

- Decreases our dependence on the reinforcement of others.

- Enables us to recognize our own areas of anger, entitlement, greed, and cowardice (given the opportunity to quietly review the day's activities and our reaction to them)

- Protects our own inner fire so that we can reach out without being pulled down.

- Helps us to accept change and loss.

- Makes us more sensitive to the compulsions in our lives.

- Allows us to experience the importance of love and acceptance (which are fruits of the contemplative life) and acknowledge the silliness and waste involved in condemning the self and judging others.

- Allows us to hear the gentle inner voice that reflects the spiritual sound of authenticity.

- Helps us respect the need to take time to strengthen our own inner space so that we can, in turn, be more sensitive to the presence of others in our lives.

In other words, taking quiet time in solitude and silence during each day can provide us with a place to breathe deeply. Yet even when we know the true value of silence and solitude, we often run from it. For us to value the quiet in our lives, we must know not only what these periods can do for us but also be able to really appreciate their price. Otherwise, we will just continue to speak about silence and solitude wistfully as something wonderful and never enjoy what this well of truth and support can offer us (Wicks, 2010).

The Pastor or Clergy Member Needs a Counselor, Too

The ability to bounce back or be resilient takes time. From my experience on the battlefield and then coming home stateside, it was incredibly difficult to go on with life without getting the necessary help to readjust to being around loved ones. The counselor or ministry professional needs a counselor as well. Gary Collins in the book *Christian Counseling* points this out and gives examples and resources:

Counselor training programs emphasize helping and caring skills. Often there is mention of warmth, empathy, and genuineness. These are three basic counselor characteristics. Counselors can get so busy in their therapeutic work that they become oblivious to professional issues or to current research that could have practical counseling implications.

(a) Conferences and seminars. Attendance at a meeting for professional counselors, pastoral counselors, lay people, or others who may consume a large block of time, but formal presentations can be helpful and often there is great value in the informal interaction with other participants.

(b) Journals. Most of these are designed for professionals and many have a specific focus, for example: *Child Development, Journal of Personality and Social Psychology*, or *Journal of Experimental Psychology*. Others such as *Journal of Psychology and Theology* or *Journal of Psychology and Christianity* have a Christian orientation and deal more often with issues that interest counselors.

(c) Books. Every year more than fifty thousand new books appear in print. Most, of course, deal with issues other than counseling, but if we add all the self-help, counseling, and psychology/psychiatry books together, there are more titles on the market than any one person can master.

Each of these resources can provide information. Many provide helpful contact with other counselors as well. The input of information from other people and resources can help keep us mentally alert, professionally stimulated, and therapeutically more effective (Collins, 1988). Work acquaintances are also difficult to get used to again due to the guilt of being away from the military deployment setting. Wicks's book helped me greatly to bounce back into regular life.

Recommendations

It is recommended that churches allow their pastors frequent time away from church to rejuvenate and rest as needed. To get good rest for a pastor means to disconnect entirely, to have no responsibilities, and if necessary, to go out of town away from congregational issues (McGarity, 2016). Annual retreats organized by different religious denominations are a possibility, and there are also various monastic retreat settings available for visitors. This would be an opportunity for clergy to recharge and to mentally prepare to apply concepts to their work.

Pastors need resources to cope with pastoral burnout, when they experience emotional exhaustion. Pastoral leaders and churches should encourage their ministers to seek out necessary resources to refresh their pastoral leadership. Despite the stress, some pastors are highly adaptive to the hardships of ministry and can demonstrate effective coping mechanisms. These pastors utilize strategies for coping with ministry stress including hobbies, spiritual development, and vacations (Anderson, 2011). The many personal issues pastors are inundated with can impact how they address and treat parishioners.

Cynicism and insensitivity, along with pessimistic attitudes toward congregants, may occur in pastors when they become burnt out. Feeling overwhelmed and exhausted leads to attempts to distance oneself emotionally and cognitively from the demands of the job. A pastor may assume an adverse attitude when working with congregants or other leaders in the church or denominational authority (Lewis, 2017) when they are burning out. Based on the data from this study, both pastors and churches should take note when pastors display signs of personal stressors. Organizations need to provide recommendations and opportunities for self-care when needed. One way of addressing this problem is to emphasize clergy health and to encourage ministers to be more intentional about implementing self-care strategies (Tan & Castillo, 2014).

It is important for pastors to take some time for mental reflection and freedom. Clergy can take advantage of daily opportunities such as being in transit, being in the backyard, or sitting in a café to replenish mental faculties. Such experiences can be immediate and require no transition time (Gill et al., 2018). Another recommendation would be for pastors to seek counseling either in a secluded professional atmosphere or in a city near the pastor's residence. I also recommend this due to potential assumptions parishioners may make and communicate with others. In this situation, the pastor would be able to talk, decompress, and learn strategies to deal with mental health. With frequent productive visits to a professional counselor, the pastor could be restored and able to lead their congregation better. Mental fatigue can be overcome, and cognitive capacity restored, by spending time in environments that allow directed attention to rest (Gill et al., 2018).

During the burnout stage, pastors deal with depression, loneliness, unresolved personal and pastoral decisions, and emotional detachment. Another suggestion would be for pastors and ministers who are dealing with depression, emotional detachment, or loneliness to learn the warning signs. Many of the warning signs manifest through internal conflicts pastors deal with concerning personal struggles in life. Employing emotional coping strategies and specific behaviors that protect against burnout is important not only for the long-term viability of the minister's career, but also the long-term health of the church (Doolittle, 2010).

Pastors need sources of support during the middle of the burnout phase. Examples of this include the utilization of ministry books, ministry manuals on burnout, and cohorts in ministry or other pastors who are their peers. It is recommended that pastors and ministers consult ministry-related materials to ascertain answers. Reaching out to cohorts and those in pastoral ministry is essential to their growth and development as well. As they reach out to peers in ministry, this mentorship can potentially assist with mental release from burnout.

Another recommendation is that pastoral staff and churches allow at least twice a year two to four weeks of paid leave for pastors to spend with their families away from the church. To reduce potential resentment from their family, it is recommended that the pastor make it a priority to ensure the vitality of their family relationships. In order for them to do this, the pastor must consistently articulate to their spouse and children that family is just as important as their commitment to their church. Healthy familial relationships provide real connections that act as a remedy for social isolation and serve to alleviate the vicarious stress of parish work (Muse et al., 2016).

While many denominations issue their pastors manuals to aid and govern their leadership in the local church, I feel that denominations do not consider the humanity of their pastors, as they, too, experience burnout at many levels. Research shows that seven out of eight pastors interviewed experienced forms of pastoral burnout. Further research would be beneficial to examine the mental health of pastoral leaders and why parishioners may find it difficult to understand the decisions they make regarding church matters. For fear of potential loss of respect in the church and the local community, the pastor may not disclose they are suffering from mental health conditions.

Further research is needed that deals with the pastor's family structure and their mental health. Clergy's mental state, if not properly adjusted before going home, may potentially bring feelings of consternation to the family. In turn, it may cause emotional discomfort in the home and send a signal to their loved ones that the job is more important than they are. Further research is also needed to address the emotional and mental scarring spouses and children experience and endure in the home due to their loved one's pastoral burnout.

Author Biography

Dr. Thomas Webb currently serves as a field grade officer and chaplain in the United States Air Force. He has spent most of his adult life in Christian ministry, in the classroom as a student learning, and, later in graduate studies, performing hundreds of hours of research in grief care and pastoral burnout. Some excerpts from his two-university post-graduate doctoral dissertations appear in this book. They were published in ProQuest Dissertations Publishing in 2015 and in 2021. The most recent one is titled "An Investigation of Pastors' Experiences During Burnout: A Case Study," published in 2021. His earlier dissertation is entitled "The Effect Grief Care to Families Has on Christian Military Chaplains," published in 2015.

He is a strong proponent of education, earning regionally accredited Doctor of Philosophy and Doctor of Ministry degrees from Amridge University in Montgomery, Alabama. He holds a Master of Divinity Degree from Lutheran Theological Seminary at Gettysburg, Pennsylvania. Earlier in his pastorate he was blessed to attain a Master of Science degree from Amridge University in Montgomery, Alabama. During his enlisted years in the military, Dr. Webb earned a Bachelor of Science degree from Faulkner University in Management of Human Resources in Montgomery, Alabama.

References

Abendroth, M., & Flannery, J. (2011). Overview and summary: Compassion fatigue: Caregivers at risk. *Online journal of issues in nursing, 16*(1), 1-3.

Bassford, V. O. (2008). *Perspectives of strength: Female elders in United Methodist ministry* (Publication No. 3323646). [Doctoral dissertation, Texas Woman's University]. ProQuest Dissertations & Theses.

Beavis, W. J. (2015). *Precipitating factors that lead to stress and burnout in restoration movement church pastors: A qualitative study* (Publication No. 3629216) [Doctoral dissertation, The Chicago School of Professional Psychology]. ProQuest Dissertations and Theses.

Brewer, E. D. (2016). *Burnout among Assemblies of God clergy with implications for support from church and denominational leaders* (Publication No. 0103257) [Doctoral dissertation, Dallas Baptist University]. ProQuest Dissertations and Theses.

Burks, S. C. (2018). *The B.R.E.A.T.H.E Self-Care Workshop* (Order No. 27736755). Available from ProQuest Dissertations & Theses Global.

Burnette, C. M. (2016). *Burnout among pastors in local church ministry in relation to pastor,congregation member, and church organizational outcomes* [Doctoral dissertation, Clemson University]. ProQuest Dissertations and Theses.

Cafferata, G. (2017). Respect, challenges, and stress among Protestant pastors closing a church:Structural and identity theory perspectives. *Pastoral Psychology, 66*(3), 311–333.

Chandler, D. J. (2009). Pastoral burnout and the impact of personal spiritual renewal, rest-taking, and support system practices. *Pastoral Psychology, 58*(3), 273–287.

Chen, D. K. (2020). *Pastoral Identity, Calling, Burnout, and Resilience* (Publication No. 22589868). [Doctoral dissertation, Fuller Theological Seminary]. ProQuest Dissertations & Theses Global.

Clay, W. R. (2019). *Clergy experiences and challenges of self-care in the church of the Nazarene* (Publication No. 2354664001) [Doctoral dissertation, Neumann University]. ProQuest Dissertations & Theses Global.

Clunan, M. B. (2016). *Factors impacting marital satisfaction within church planter marriages in the United States* (Publication No. 1845890992). [Doctoral dissertation, New Orleans Baptist Theological Seminary]. ProQuest Dissertations & Theses Global: Psychology Database.

Coates, B. (2019). *Worthy of Double Honor: An Examination of Employee Development Methods Used for Paid Ministerial Staff in SBC 500 Churches* (Publication No. 27665969). [Doctoral dissertation, Southeastern Baptist Theological Seminary]. ProQuest Dissertations & Theses Global.

Collins, Gary R. Christian Counseling. Dallas: Word Publishing, 1988.

Coy, J. S., Lambert, J. E., & Miller, M. M. (2016). Stories of the accused: A phenomenological inquiry of MFTs and inquiry of accusations of unprofessional conduct. *Journal of Marital and Family Therapy, 42*(1), 139–152.

Doolittle, B. R. (2010). The impact of behaviors upon burnout among parish-based clergy. *Journal of Religion and Health, 49*(1), 88–95.

Els, C., Mostert, K., & de Beer, L. T. (2015). Job characteristics, burnout, and the relationship with recovery experiences. *SA Journal of Industrial Psychology, 41*(1), 1–13.

Exantus, W. R. (2011). *Pastoral burnout and leadership styles: A mixed-methods study of southern baptist pastors in central florida* (Publication No. 3443660). [Doctoral dissertation, Capella University]. ProQuest Dissertations & Theses Global

Figley, C. R. (2013). Compassion fatigue: Coping with secondary traumatic stress disorder in those who treat the traumatized. Routledge.

Flatt, B. W. (1987). *Growing Through Grief.* Christian Communications.

Frederick, T. V., Dunbar, S., & Thai, Y. (2018). Burnout in Christian perspective. *Pastoral Psychology, 67*(3), 267–276.

Gildner, D. D. (2016). *Practicing sabbath: Improving clergy health and helping differentiate one's self from role, preventing one cause of clergy* (Publication No. 10970392) [Doctoral dissertation, United Theological Seminary]. ProQuest Dissertations & Theses Global.

Gill, C., Packer, J., & Ballantyne, R. (2018). Applying attention restoration theory to understand and address clergy's need to restore cognitive capacity. *Journal of Religion and Health, 57*(5), 1779–1792.

Hanley, T. C. E. (2019). *Compassion fatigue, self-care, and clergy members: How social workers can help* [Master's thesis, California State University, San Bernardino].

Harper, D. D. R. (2017). *The Love-Empowered Leader: A Qualitative Case Study of a Pastoral Leadership Exemplar of an Evangelical Congregation in*

Virginia (Publication No. 10601057) [Doctoral dissertation, Regent University]. ProQuest Dissertations and Theses.

Harris, H., & LMSW-ACP, D. C. S. W. (2003). What Is a Congregation to Do? Grief in Family Congregational Life. *Journal of Family Ministry, 17*, 12-27.

Hebden, I. (2020). *The avoidance of burnout among Open Bible pastors: Creating healthy andvibrant leaders in ministry.* [Doctoral dissertation, George Fox University].

Heck, A., Drumm, R., McBride, D., & Sedlacek, D. (2018). Seventh-day Adventist clergy: Understanding stressors and coping mechanisms. *Review of Religious Research, 60*(1), 115–132.

Hessel, V. E. Jr. (2015). *Phenomenological study of pastor burnout* (Publication No. 3692076) [Doctoral dissertation, University of Phoenix]. ProQuest Dissertations and Theses.

Hester, J. A. (2018). *Stress and longevity in pastoral ministry: A phenomenological study.* [Doctoral dissertation, The Southern Baptist Theological Seminary].

Hoover, J. (2021). *The Predictive Value of Coping Factors on Emotional Exhaustion in Ministry* [Doctoral dissertation, Grand Canyon University]. (Publication No. 28541756). ProQuest Dissertations & Theses Global.

Hough, H., Proeschold-Bell, R., Liu, X., Weisner, C., Turner, E. L., & Yao, J. (2019). Relationships between sabbath observance and mental, physical, and spiritual health in clergy. *Pastoral Psychology, 68*(2), 171–193.

Jackson-Jordan, E. A. (2013). Clergy burnout and resilience: A review of the literature. *Journal of Pastoral Care and Counseling, 67*(1), 1–5. (Publication No. 3685807)

[Doctoral dissertation, The University of North Carolina at Charlotte].

Jackson, K. L. (2017). *A qualitative study understanding the perceptions of Black Pentecostal pastors towards mental health and collaborating with mental health counselors* [Doctoral dissertation, Ohio University].

Joiner, A. V. (2020). *Perceptions of burnout among black pastors of small churches: A phenomenological study* (Publication No. 28027135). [Doctoral dissertation, University of Missouri-Kansas City]. Available from ProQuest Dissertations & Theses Global.

Joinson, C. (1992). Coping with compassion fatigue. *Nursing, 22* (4), 116-118.

Kalish, R. (1981). *Death, Grief, And Caring Relationships,* 301. Monterey: Brooks/Cole Publishing Company.

Koo, B. C. (2017). *Pastoral Burnout and Sabbatical Leave* (Publication No. 10639242). [Doctoral dissertation, Biola University]. ProQuest Dissertations & Theses Global. Available from ProQuest Dissertations & Theses Global.

Lebo, D. (2020). *Understanding contributing factors of burnout in United Methodist clergy.* (Publication No. 27832867) [Doctoral dissertation, Alvernia University]. ProQuest Dissertations & Theses Global.

Lewis, H. D. S., Sr. (2017). *A phenomenological study of religious pastors at risk for burnout*(Publication No. 2008659561) [Doctoral dissertation, The University of the Rockies]. ProQuest Dissertations & Theses Global: Psychology Database.

Louw, D. (2015). Compassion fatigue: Spiritual exhaustion and the cost of caring in the pastoral ministry, towards a 'pastoral diagnosis' in caregiving. *Hervormde Teologiese Studies, 71*(2), 1–10.

Marcena, A. A. (2018). *Minimizing leadership burnout through the practice of self-care* (Publication No. 10970397).) [Doctoral dissertation, United Theological Seminary]. ProQuest Dissertations & Theses Global.

Maslach, C., & Jackson, S. E. (1981). The measurement of experienced burnout. *Journal of organizational behavior, 2*(2), 99-113.

Miller, A. M. (2014) *Beating Burnout: A 30-Day Guide to Hope and Health* (Carol Stream: Tyndale House Publishers, 2014): 40-42.

McGarity, J. H. (2016). *Identifying characteristics of pastoral burnout in local church ministry* (Publication No. 10245377). [Doctoral dissertation, Biola University]. ProQuest Dissertations & Theses Global; Religion Database.

Millikin, R. (2018). *Never alone: Discovering the path to burnout avoidance.* [Doctoral dissertation, George Fox University].

Miner, M. H., Dowson, M., & Sterland, S. (2010). Ministry orientation and ministry outcomes: Evaluation of a new multidimensional model of clergy burnout and job satisfaction. *Journal of Occupational and Organizational Psychology, 83*(1), 167–188.

Muse S., Love, M., & Christensen, K. (2016). Intensive outpatient therapy for clergy burnout: How much difference can a week make? *Journal of Religion and Health, 55* (1), 147–158.

Only, E. D. (2021). A Practical Intervention for the Solo Pastor (Publication No. 28413583). [Doctoral dissertation,

Virginia Union University]. ProQuest Dissertations & Theses.

Pickett, C. C., Barrett, J. L., Eriksson, C. B., & Kabiri, C. (2017). Social networks among ministry relationships: Relational capacity, burnout, & ministry effectiveness. Journal of *Psychology and Theology, 45* (2), 92–105.

Ream, S. T. (2016). *Pastoral health and burnout: Spiritual maturity, emotional health, andphysical environment* (Publication No. 1862201777) [Doctoral dissertation, Nyack College, Alliance Theological Seminary]. ProQuest Dissertations and Theses.

Rokach, A. (2018). Effective coping with loneliness: A review. *Open Journal of Depression, 7*(4), 61–72.

Rosales, A. I. (2019). *Clergy Wellbeing: The Role of Lived Values and Values Fit* (Publication No. 22621875).) [Doctoral dissertation, Fuller Theological Seminary]. ProQuest Dissertations & Theses Global.

Saakvitne, K. W., & Pearlman, L. A. (1996). *Transforming the pain: A workbook on vicarious traumatization.* WW Norton & Co.

Schaefer, A. G., & Jacobsen, S. (2009). Surviving clergy burnout. *Encounter, 70*(1), 37–66.

Schaufeli, W. B., Leiter, M. P., & Maslach, C. (2009). Burnout: 35 years of research and practice. *Career development international.*

Scott, G., & Lovell, R. (2015). The rural pastor's initiative: Addressing isolation and burnout in rural ministry. *Pastoral Psychology, 64*(1), 71–97.

Sixbey, B. K. (2014). *Clergy peer groups: Do they make a difference for clergy health?* (Publication No. 3684665)

[Doctoral dissertation, Asbury Theological Seminary]. ProQuest Dissertations and Theses.

Snelgar, R. J., Renard, M., & Shelton, S. (2017). Preventing compassion fatigue amongst pastors: The influence of spiritual intelligence and intrinsic motivation. *Journal of Psychology and Theology, 45*(4), 247–260.

Soto, L. A. (2015). *Team approach to ministry: Effective strategy against pastoral burnout.* [Doctoral dissertation, Asbury Theological Seminary].

Speight, D. E., & Speight, S. W. (2017). Exploring the lived experience of forced termination among Southern Baptist clergy couples: A retrospective study. *Journal of Psychology and Christianity, 36*(2), 149–160.

Stephens, N. M. (2020). *A correlational study of burnout and personality among clergy in the United States* (Publication No. 2395299907) [Doctoral dissertation, Nathanael M. Andrews University]. ProQuest Dissertations & Theses Global.

Streets, F. (2015). Social work and a trauma-informed ministry and pastoral care: A collaborative agenda. *Social Work and Christianity, 42*(4), 470–487.

Stewart, D. W. (2012). Compassion fatigue: what is the level among army chaplains? Journal of Workplace Behavioral Health, 27(1), 1-11.

Strong, R. (2017). *Pastoral burnout among African American pastors: A Biblical and practical solution.* [Doctoral dissertation, Liberty University School of Divinity].

Tan, S., & Castillo, M. (2014). Self-care and beyond: A brief literature review from a Christian perspective. *Journal of Psychology and Christianity, 33*(1), 90–95.

Tanner, M. N., & Zvonkovic, A. M. (2011). Forced to leave: Forced termination. experiences of Assemblies of God clergy and its connection to stress and well-being outcomes. *Pastoral Psychology, 60*(5), 713–726.

Trihub, B. L., McMinn, M. R., Buhrow, W. C., Jr., & Johnson, T. F. (2010). Denominational support for clergy mental health. *Journal of Psychology and Theology, 38*(2), 101–110.

Tyson, J. (2007). Compassion fatigue in the treatment of combat-related trauma during wartime. *Clinical Social Work Journal, 35,* 183-192.

Visker, J. D., Rider, T., & Humphers-Ginther, A. (2017). Ministry-related burnout and stress coping mechanisms among Assemblies of God-ordained clergy in Minnesota. *Journal of Religion and Health, 56*(3), 951–961.

White, S. D. (2020). Ministerial Training on Consumer Culture and Volunteer Management May Prevent Burnout for Small-Church Clergy. *Pastoral Psychology, 69*(3), 225-248.

Williams, D. R. (2019). *Phenomenological study of encouragement as a protective factor for new Christian pastors* (Publication No. 13903419) [Doctoral dissertation, Grand Canyon University]. ProQuest Dissertations and Theses.

Milton Keynes UK
Ingram Content Group UK Ltd.
UKHW052245220424
441436UK00007BA/50

9 798989 643479